Rockets and Astronauts

Rockets and Astronauts

by Brenda Thompson
and
Rosemary Giesen

illustrated by
David Hardy and Rosemary Giesen

Lerner Publications Company
Minneapolis

Original text by Brenda Thompson
Revised text by Rosemary Giesen
Illustrations by David Hardy
Additional drawings by Rosemary Giesen

LIBRARY OF CONGRESS CATALOGING IN PUBLICATION DATA

Thompson, Brenda.
Rockets and astronauts.

(A First Fact Book)
SUMMARY: Traces the development of astronautics from
the first unmanned artificial satellite through lunar landings
to plans for space stations and extensive space travel.

1. Astronautics—Juvenile literature. [1. Astronautics] I. Giesen, Rosemary, joint author. II. Hardy, David A. III. Title.

TL793.T468 1977 E 629.47   76-22453
ISBN 0-8225-1360-9

Manufactured in the United States of America

International Standard Book Number: 0-8225-1360-9
Library of Congress Catalog Card Number: 76-22453

1 2 3 4 5 6 7 8 9 10 85 84 83 82 81 80 79 78 77

The space age began on October 4, 1957, when Russia launched *Sputnik I.* It was the first artificial satellite to circle the earth. A satellite is an object in space that moves in a path, called an *orbit,* around a larger object. The first person to travel in space was Yuri A. Gagarin of Russia. On April 12, 1961, he orbited the earth once. Russians who travel in space are called *cosmonauts.* Alan Shepard became the first American space traveler on May 5, 1961. Americans who travel and work in space are called *astronauts.* Astronaut means "sailor among the stars."

Many astronauts take part in a space mission. Some stay on the ground. Some work in space. Astronauts find out more about the earth, moon, and stars.

In order for astronauts to reach space, they must overcome gravity. Gravity is the force that pulls things to earth. Only rockets have enough power to overcome gravity and lift people into space.

This *Saturn V* rocket carries astronauts to the moon. A machine called a *crawler* takes the spacecraft, the rocket, and its launch tower to the launch pad.

Ten, nine, eight, seven, six, five, four, three, two, one, zero! The countdown ends. Rocket engines fire. The rocket lifts off.

To overcome the earth's gravity, the spacecraft must be pushed faster and faster. A lot of fuel must be burned to give enough speed. The fuel is carried in rockets stacked one on top of the other. These rocket parts are called *stages*. The Saturn V rocket has three stages. As the spacecraft moves away from the earth, the lower stages burn up their fuel. Then they drop away. Now the spacecraft is lighter and can move faster.

When the last stage falls away, the spacecraft is moving at 24,300 miles (39,110 kilometers) an hour.

Six minutes after lift-off, the spacecraft
reaches space. Space begins about 100
miles (160 kilometers) above the earth. The
force of gravity is much less here than it
is close to the earth.

Strange things happen in space where there is little gravity. People and things have no weight. They will float around unless they are strapped down.

In space there is no air, food, or water. Astronauts must carry these things with them. They eat food out of tubes. Astronauts cannot eat with spoons in space!

Astronauts can leave their spacecraft and "walk" in space. Outside the spacecraft they must wear spacesuits. They use a gas gun to move around. If they fire the gun one way, they move the other way.

Astronauts can also land on the moon.
There they travel around in a lunar rover. It
moves easily over low rocks and thick dust.

When the astronauts are ready to leave
the moon, they use a rocket to lift off. The
moon is smaller than the earth, so it has
much less gravity. A small rocket can lift the
spacecraft off the moon.

When the spacecraft rushes back to earth, the air slows it down like a giant brake. The air that rushes around the spacecraft becomes very hot.

A spacecraft carries big parachutes that open 10,000 feet (3,000 meters) above the earth. The parachutes float the spacecraft slowly down. It usually lands in the ocean.

In the future, several countries may share a space station that would orbit the earth. The station would be a space lab and a place for spacecraft to refuel.

People dream about going to the stars.
Today we have no means to travel so far.
But in the future, strange new spacecraft
may be built to go far into space.

More About Rockets and Astronauts

Two kinds of spacecraft explore space but do not carry astronauts. They are artificial satellites and space probes.

There are many kinds of artificial satellites. Weather satellites take pictures of the earth. Scientists look at these pictures to see how weather develops.

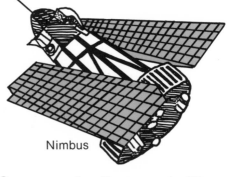

Nimbus

Communications satellites send telephone, television, and radio signals from one part of the world to another.

Telestar

Space probes explore the moon, planets, and space near the earth and far away. Space probes take pictures. They can be used to prepare for later exploration by astronauts.

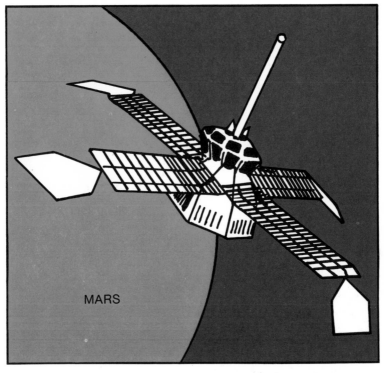

MARS

Mariner Space Probe

List of New Words

artificial satellite

astronaut

cosmonaut

crawler

gravity

lunar rover

orbit

parachute

Saturn V rocket

space probe

Sputnik I

stage

A Message to Educators

Children who have just learned to read have entered a world filled with new pleasure and knowledge. They have begun a journey that will take them to distant times, to far-away lands, and to the mysterious territory inside their own minds. The *First Fact Books* are designed to help young readers get a good start on that life-long journey. Originally conceived by Brenda Thompson, a British educator and author, the series provides a first look at a variety of topics drawn from the fields of science and history. Each book makes use of vivid, full-color illustrations that serve to attract and hold the young reader's interest. The simply written text satisfies that interest by presenting basic facts about the subject in a manner that is both stimulating and informative. In addition, each book includes a section containing supplementary information for those readers who want to expand their knowledge. Designed for both classroom use and independent study, the *First Fact Books* provide children with an early learning experience that is both enjoyable and rewarding.